A SNOWSTORM
SHOWS OFF

BLIZZARDS

BELINDA JENSEN

illustrations by **Renée Kurilla**

series consultant: Lisa Bullard

M Millbrook Press/Minneapolis

To Dan Gavin, Doug, Don, Bob, Dana, Sharon, Jane, and my cowriter Lisa: I feel so blessed to have all of you mentors through the years. Thank you all for helping me navigate a path that is so enjoyable. —B.J.

For my husband, Keith—the best person to be snowed in with! —R.K.

Millbrook Press
A division of Lerner Publishing Group, Inc.
241 First Avenue North
Minneapolis, MN 55401 USA

For reading levels and more information, look up this title at www.lernerbooks.com.

Snowflake background: © Nikiteev Konstantin/Shutterstock.com.

Main body text set in ChurchwardSamoa Regular 15/18.
Typeface provided by Chank.

Library of Congress Cataloging-in-Publication Data

Jensen, Belinda. author.
  A Snowstorm Shows Off: Blizzards / by Belinda Jensen ; Renée Kurilla, illustrator.
     pages cm — (Bel the Weather Girl)
  Includes bibliographical references and index.
  Audience: 005-007.
  Audience: K to Grade 3.
  ISBN 978-1-4677-7961-6 (lb : alk. paper) — ISBN 978-1-4677-9743-6 (pb : alk. paper) —
ISBN 978-1-4677-9744-3 (eb pdf)
  1. Blizzards—Juvenile literature. 2. Severe storms—Juvenile literature. I. Kurilla, Renée. illustrator. II. Title.
QC926.37.J46 2016
 551.55'5—dc23
                                             2015015836

Manufactured in the United States of America
1 - CG - 12/31/15

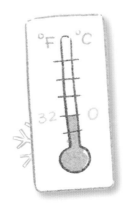

TABLE OF CONTENTS

Chapter One
So Much Snow!

"WOW! That's a lot of snow." Bel's cousin Dylan shook snow off his coat. "Your mom's forecast said we'd only get a little!"

Dress warmly to stay safe in cold weather. Remember your hat and mittens. Wear a coat and snow pants to keep your clothes dry.

"Mom says snowstorms are sneaky," Bel said.

"Even meteorologists don't always know how hard they'll hit—or where."

"Let's talk about snow science!" Their teacher, Mr. Gavin, held up a cup. "Sometimes water is liquid. Sometimes water is a vapor we can't see."

It snows in all fifty states of the United States. It even snows in Hawaii!

He pointed outside. "When water vapor gets cold enough, it freezes. It turns into ice crystals high in the air. The crystals fall as snow."

Mr. Gavin wrote on the board: "Water freezes at 32° Fahrenheit (0° Celsius)." Then a big gust of wind rattled the windows. "Take a wiggle break," he said. "I need to call the office."

Everyone rushed to look outside. Snow was blowing everywhere! Bel couldn't even see the playground.

9

Chapter Two
A Blizzard Begins

Mr. Gavin hung up. "Back to your seats. The storm seems to be turning into a blizzard. But we're perfectly safe."

"What if we get a mountain of snow?" Cody yelled. "We could be stuck here until summer!"

"I'm scared! I want my mom." Lily looked ready to cry.

11

Bel raised her hand. "Hold on! Weather isn't so scary once you understand it!"

"That's right," said Mr. Gavin. "And we have a weather expert in our class. Bel, come on up here. Explain to everybody about blizzards."

Blizzards are winter storms where the wind gusts at least 35 miles (56 kilometers) per hour. The gusts keep happening for at least three hours. Lots of falling or blowing snow makes it hard to see.

Bel bumped her fists together. "Warm air and cold air don't get along," she said. "When they meet, the wind gets stronger. In a blizzard, that strong wind blows snow around like crazy."

Dylan said, "So a blizzard is just a show-off snowstorm!"

Bel nodded. "But not all snowstorms are blizzards. Blizzards need big winds."

"I wish we'd gone home before it started!" said Lily.

Blizzards always include blowing snow. But new snow doesn't always fall during these storms. In ground blizzards, the wind blows around snow already on the ground.

"But we don't always know blizzards are coming," Bel said.
"And they can whip up fast."

Chapter Three
The Blizzard Party

Mr. Gavin stood up. "Great job, Bel! Now, who wants to go to a blizzard party in the gym?"

The whole school came to the party. Bel was blizzard hopscotch champion.

To be safe, stay inside during blizzard conditions. Keep blizzard supplies on hand during the winter. These include bottled water, flashlights, blankets, a radio, and extra batteries.

Finally, the principal whistled for quiet. "The wind is dying down. Plows are clearing the streets. It won't be long before we can go home."

17

Lily looked at Bel. "You said a blizzard can happen fast. What if it starts again before my mom gets here?"

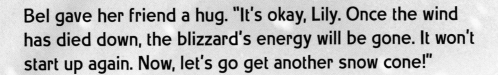

Bel gave her friend a hug. "It's okay, Lily. Once the wind has died down, the blizzard's energy will be gone. It won't start up again. Now, let's go get another snow cone!"

In 1993 a blizzard called the Storm of the Century hit twenty-six states. One town in Tennessee recorded 5 feet (1.5 meters) of snow. Winds gusted over 70 miles (113 km) per hour.

Lily's mom walked in while Lily was showing Bel her purple tongue. "Guess what, Mom?" said Lily. "Bel taught us all about blizzards today. She really is Bel the Weather Girl! Do you think we'll have a snow day tomorrow, Bel?"

"I hope so," answered Bel. "But stay tuned.
**Because every day is another
weather day!"**

Try It: Make Play Snow

With an adult, you can mix simple household ingredients to make your own play snow!

What you will need:

About 3 cups of baking soda

Large bowl or pan

½ cup to 1 cup of white-colored hand lotion, depending on the desired consistency

(It's okay to start with less baking soda—then just use less lotion.)

What to do:

Put the baking soda in a large bowl or pan. Slowly add a little bit of lotion. Mix them together with your hands. Do you notice that your mixture feels a little cold? Keep mixing in small amounts of lotion until your play snow feels like real snow. It should be wet enough that you can roll it into snowballs, but not too wet. To make snow that packs together even more easily, you can also add a little water to the mix. Once your snow is ready, you can make a snowperson or a mini snow fort.

When you are done, put your snow in a sealed container or baggie for another day of play!

Glossary

blizzard: a winter storm with winds gusting at least 35 miles (56 km) per hour and blowing snow making it difficult to see more than one-quarter of a mile (0.4 km) for three hours or more

crystals: a solid material made of a regularly repeating pattern

gust: a strong rush of wind

liquid: a substance in a flowing form, such as oil or water

meteorologists: people who are trained to study and predict the weather

vapor: a substance in the form of a gas

weather forecast: a prediction of weather conditions based on science and technology

Further Reading

Books

Bullard, Lisa. *Blizzards.* Minneapolis: Lerner Publications, 2009.
In this book, you can learn more facts about blizzards and see photos of these winter storms.

Cassino, Mark. *The Story of Snow: The Science of Winter's Wonder.* San Francisco: Chronicle, 2009.
This book will teach you more about the science of snow while showing you close-up photos of snow crystals.

Rocco, John. *Blizzard.* New York: Disney-Hyperion, 2014.
Read a true story about one boy's adventure during a blizzard.

Websites

BrainPOP: Snowflakes
http://www.brainpop.com/science/weather/snowflakes
Watch this cartoon to learn more about snowflakes.

NOAA: Winter Storms
http://www.nws.noaa.gov/om/brochures/owlie/Owlie-winter.pdf
You can color these pages while you learn more about winter storms.

Winter Storms/Extreme Cold
http://www.ready.gov/kids/know-the-facts/winter-storms-extreme-cold
Learn more about staying safe in winter storms.

Index

LERNER
e
SOURCE

Expand learning beyond the printed book. Download free, complementary educational resources for this book from our website, www.lerneresource.com.

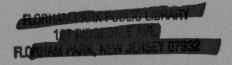